To: Kat Ja
Thanks for your support..
Keep on #Stepping Out on Faith
Dare to Dream

STEPPING OUT
ON FAITH:
Dare to Dream

A Jour

Gladys "Peaches" Kenney

Gladys Peaches Kenney

Stepping Out on
Faith Dare to Dare
www.FaithSteps8.com

Stepping Out on Faith Dare to Dream: A Journal of Faith Copyright © 2016 by Gladys "Peaches" Kenney

First Edition: November 2016 Baltimore, MD

All rights reserved. Printed in the United States of America. No part of this book may be used or reproduced in any manner whatsoever without written permission except in the case of brief quotations embodied in critical articles or reviews. This book is a work of real life, personal experiences in faith. Names, characters, businesses, organizations and places really exist. Only in some instances were names changed to protect the privacy of the other party(ies) involved in my life.

For information contact email FaithSteps8@gmail.com or visit our website http://faithsteps8.wixsite.com/soof

Book and Cover design by Annette Miller

Editors Annette Miller & Tiara S. Carr

ISBN-13: 978-1539788867

~~~~~~~~~~~~~~~~~~~~~~~~~~~~~~~~~

Written in memory of:

My eldest brother,
Anthony J. Rhem
(November 17, 1969-April 1996)

&

My first husband,
C. Matthew Kenney aka "Whiteboy Matt Kenney"

(June 9, 1972 - October 2001)

Table of Contents

Acknowledgements

I first would like to thank God for allowing this book to be released after years of it lying dormant. Also, I want to thank my close family and friends especially, Renetha, Rosette, Shirl, Courtney, Pastor Ayo, Monica, Kishia, Katuhra, who believed in me and encouraged me along the way.

To my mother and father for giving birth to me: Mom, I pray this book will ignite a fire within you to fulfill your dreams and passions. You have given to everyone, but now it is time for you to spoil yourself. You are an intelligent woman and other women need to know how you survived the things you did in your marriage. English is one of your favorite subjects, so writing, which you used to love, should come natural for you. As the title reads, Stepping Out on Faith. You can do all things but fail with Christ. It is time to live life to the fullest. Mom, thank you so much for sending us to church as children and teaching us the Word of God. Although I strayed during puberty, the Word of God drew me back to Him. Dad, thanks for your great cooking, laughter, and dancing. Also, Dad thanks for giving me bottles of water after I minister in dance.

Thank you Apostle Dr. Karen S. Bethea, (my beautiful pastor) for living a life of integrity and being an open display of what God will and can do in and through your life when you yield to His will. Apostle Karen, your walk is encouraging to me and your sermons and books helped to birth this baby out. There are more to come. As the theme for the Spa Retreat 2015 said, "This Girl is on Fire," and I am going to keep my charge. Thank you again.

Thank you to my new mentor, Janean Stubbs-Taylor, author of Fruits of Finance. You have not only embraced me but allowed God to use you by becoming my Author Midwife while I was in labor with this book. Although we did not know each other in all trimesters, God allowed our paths to cross at the right appointed time when these books were ready in the birth canal. Although I delayed the process with procrastination and sometimes fear, I believe God used you to help induce my labor at the 2015 Spa Retreat when you spoke into my spirit "PUSH and PERSEVERE because the world needs what [I] have!" I was slain in the spirit yet God showed me in the spirit realm that I would be giving birth to several books in this physical world. I cannot thank you enough for your Prophetic Affirmation and confirmation spoken in my life. God did a seasonal shifting in the spirit and natural.

Last but not least, I definitely thank my editor, Annette "Netty" Miller, for initially standing in agreement with me the moment I shared my project with you. You stepped right in at the very beginning ready to assist me with the task at hand. Initially you were passive but your approach became more direct when you declared a deadline of May 2015, and at that moment my faith became a little rocky. However, I agreed and added my faith to your faith. We met and I saw God's power manifest as we worked on the book and more ideas flourished. The Spa Retreat 2015 sealed the deal. After all of the guests left, I sat in the lobby and focused on finishing this book.

I had a vendor table to promote Stepping Out on Faith Dare to Dream: A Journal of Faith at the next "Women Who Soar" event in November 2016. I made this declaration by faith for the past three years. It finally happened. There is power in your words. Speak Life!

"Walk into your God given Purpose."

~GPK~ Author

Foreword

"Every once in a while someone takes a pen and chronicles their journey. In doing so they bless those who can relate, those who needed to hear their story, and those coming behind them who need the courage to face what they have overcome. In her first book, Gladys "Peaches" Kenney, transparently shares her journey of faith and courage with us. May you be encouraged as you read her journey of faith!"

~Dr. Karen S. Bethea
Senior Pastor
Set the Captives Free Outreach Center
Baltimore, Maryland

~~~   ~~~   ~~~   ~~~

"Stepping Out on Faith Dare to Dream" is a book about trusting God with all your heart. Gladys Kenney is a dynamic woman of Faith with a heart to see men and women of God walk in their God given purpose. Gladys takes us on a journey to discover what true faith really means through a process led solely by God.

This powerful book is written with transparency, encouragement, and spiritual insights that will challenge readers to stand firm on God's word. Stepping Out on Faith Dare to Dream follows the blue print for Christian living."

Pastor Ayo Thomas
Founder of WOE Magazine

Introduction

What does it mean to STEP Out on FAITH? What is Faith? I am glad you asked. According to Google, the definition of Faith is "1. Complete confidence in someone or something 2. Strong belief in God or in the doctrines of a religion, based on spiritual apprehension rather than proof. According to the Bible, "faith is the substance of things hoped for and the evidence of things not seen" (Hebrews 11:1). "But without faith it is impossible to please him: for he that cometh to God must believe that he is, and that he is a rewarder of them that diligently seek him." (Hebrews 11:6).

Having faith means that you believe God despite the circumstances surrounding you. I will be honest, there will be times that you appear "crazy" or "like you lost your mind," but you need to stand on the Word of God. In addition, you need to make sure that you are spending quality time in the Word and attending a Bible- believing church where you can be edified in your spirit. Faith comes by hearing, and hearing by the Word of God. As the preacher preaches the Word, there should be confirmation of what God has already spoken to you. I welcome you to Step Out on Faith with me as I share moments in my life where I learned to walk by faith and not by sight.

My starting point for writing this book occurred in 2012. This book captures different phases of my life in which I openly share about my personal, spiritual, and emotional experiences. You will learn about the good and life=changing choices that I have made. Also, you will learn about my complicated process writing this book. Different levels of my faith were revealed through my personal journal entries. Throughout the book, I am very expressive to how I feel about God and I show my admiration and gratitude towards Him in what I call {Glory Breaks}. Let me warn you that they appear frequently. Please note some of the journal entries are intertwined while others can stand alone. What integrates the stories into one is how I share the process of writing this book over the course of four years. The goal is to compel you to want to write your own story. Everyone has a message to share.

Also, it is to teach you how to walk by faith and not by sight while trusting God. In addition, I hope you to learn from my experiences and the positive choices that I made. If you can glean from them, feel free. But please try to avoid some of my pitfalls I encountered. Lastly, Stepping Out on Faith Dare to Dream: A Journal of Faith was created to inspire you to use your God-given talents to pursue your own dreams.

The Starting Line

Journal Entry: Spa Retreat

"For I am confident of this very thing, that He who began a good work in you will perfect it until the day of Christ Jesus" (Philippians 1:6)

It was a beautiful sunny weekend in York, Pennsylvania in May 2012. I was away to enjoy the Spa Retreat Women's Conference. I was full of excitement because I knew that God was going to do some amazing things. For instance, I was taking notes from the workshops which converted into something bigger. The pen hit the paper and the journaling commenced for this book.

WHOLE was the theme of the conference. God was putting all the pieces together in us to make us whole again. Apostle Dr. Karen Bethea was the speaker and although her notes were lost in her laptop which died, it did not stop God from moving. I recall thinking, "Wow, Lord you are taking me from glory to glory. This retreat is about me applying Your Word for real. I must take the limits off of God and truly exercise my Faith." Have you ever limited God by assuming your problem was too BIG for Him to solve? That night God showed His favor. As I went to purchase the most creatively hand-made fans from two vendors, (www.uniquelyyouandme.vpweb.com & www.mysunnycreations.com), for my mother and bless my two dear sisters Renetha and Shirl, God appeared to be setting me up to be blessed by Him. It was through the power of giving. The Bible says when you give and it shall be given to you, pressed down shaken together and men shall give to your bosom (Luke 6:38). While shopping for my mom and sisters, I saw a blue journal which read, "New Mercies

Everyday Great is Thy Faithfulness." Wow, I had to buy that because, one, that was one of my favorite songs the Lord had me minister to for years. And secondly, it was my favorite color, I thought. "Surely, it will be used to write many notes, books, stories, testimonies, and prayers."

Later that night during my reflection time, I sat basking in the presence of God. As I meditated, God gave me the outline for this book. I began to write down the chapters of Stepping Out on Faith. I recall feeling very happy when I went to bed.

The next day of the retreat as I was talking with my friend and she shared that she and her mother were in the process of buying their own homes. I shouted, "Glory!" and I thought, "I am next in line; my time is coming." I claimed by faith I would be buying my house within a few days because I had been shopping around for a house with my realtor." I got into the habit of saying "Thank you, Jesus" in advance. I claimed a deck, nice garage, and three or four bedrooms. And I believed it would come to pass. As I spoke with my friend, it was exciting to hear about God opening up doors for His children. My spirit was being fed and my faith was increasing.

Later I took time to write in my journal and I looked at the different chapters of the book again. Meanwhile, in my reflection time, the Lord reminded me that He had already blessed me with the gift of writing. He reminded me of when I wrote two poems, one dedicated to Him on Valentine's Day in 1998 and one about Humility a few years later. In addition, I often wrote very encouraging notes and cards to family and friends to uplift their spirits.

{GLORY BREAKS} Thank You Jesus for this day. Thank

You for my life. Thank You for who You are: Sovereign, Worthy, King of Kings, Counselor, Mind Regulator, My Peace, My Protector, My Provider, My Guide, My Comforter, My Answer, My Healer, My Strength, My Joy, My Favor, and My Tower. My ALL! ....Who is God to you? {Selah}

During the last day of the retreat, I was so overjoyed from the night before that I did not sleep long. I woke earlier than I normally do. It was about 4:30 in the morning when I was communing with God, reading his Word, and writing in my journal. It was then that He spoke in my spirit that I would write books. Then a few hours later during the retreat service, the preacher was speaking her message then she spoke, "God said 'You will write books.'" She stated "God said you would write five books." When she said this, I literally ran around the conference room praising God. That was truly confirmation of God revealing and reminding me that I was on track and should get to writing. During my quiet time with God, He spoke to my spirit and later used the preacher to confirmed what He said, but with more detail. Now I know that I will be writing at least four more books. At this point in my life, I am aware of what three of the books will be about, but the last one is a mystery for now until the Lord reveals it. Please note: this book was written in parts since all was not revealed at once. For example, I did not write the story then the title the chapters. Quite the opposite; God gave me the chapters before I even started writing. The most important thing I needed to do was to act in faith and Step out. And the Writing began....

Something to Think About: *God gives instructions and He usually confirms what He speaks through His word. What was the last instruction He gave you to follow? Has He confirmed it? What do you need to begin? What steps do you need to take? Are you worrying about the resources you need? Use what resources you have and the rest will follow.*

Journal Entry: Procrastination

Diligent hands will rule, but laziness ends in
forced labor.
(Proverbs 12:24)

Have you delayed completing an assignment, chore, and/or job to do something more pleasurable? If you are like me, then we have walked down the same road. We have procrastinated. The Merriam-Webster Dictionary defines procrastination as "to be slow or late about doing something that should be done: to delay doing something until a later time because you do not want to do it, because you are lazy, etc."

But, truly I think that my name Gladys "Peaches" Kenney, could have been listed right there at times. Procrastination is the silent killer of dreams, motivation, progression, purpose, destiny and all things that can push you to a better future. It makes even the best intentions look bad. Although I started writing my book, my poor habit of procrastination crept in and I got off task. In the world of procrastination, one puts off now to do later, but later may never come since time waits for no man. It is weird knowing that tasks do need to be completed, no matter how great or small, and no matter how much you push it to the side to avoid it. Meanwhile, you may try to do other deeds or busy work as an excuse for why you did not complete the assignment, however God, your parents, spouse, supervisor, teacher, friend, pastor, and, etc. will expect it to be done. "Ouch!!!" Well, I am stepping on own toes because I am guilty as charged. I was not disciplining myself with my deadlines. I was putting off writing the book.

Thus, it took longer to complete this goal, while others around me were coming out with their new books. My level of maturity allowed me to celebrate my friends for their accomplishments, and gave me the nudge I needed to get to writing again. In case you are struggling with procrastination, then shake that spirit off because it is not like God. Repent and pray for another opportunity and be prepared the next time.

Prayer: Lord please forgive me for the many times I procrastinated to obey your directions. Help me to learn to obey your voice. Renew me and cleanse me from all unrighteousness. Please help me to remain motivated. Thank you for another chance to im*prove.*

Something to Think About: *What is it you need to do or complete that will bring you peace once it's done? I challenge you to pray for God's grace and motivation to tackle it and push past the distractions. Stop procrastinating: you can do it.*

Journal Entry: Great is Thy Faithfulness

"It is of the Lord's mercies that we are not consumed, because His compassions fail not."
(Lamentations 3:21-23)

One day I was commuting home from work, and I reflecting on God's goodness. I thought, "I am amazed how
God is so faithful. Great is thy Faithfulness!"

He is truly good and that's an understatement. I was
thinking, "Wow! I'm literally writing this book on the MARC
train leaving DC." God had my fingers and brain moving
so fast that I was in awe of what He doing and using me to
do during that time. I had maximized the moment.

I am humbled yet trying to maintain my composure
as I reflect on His faithfulness. I am so glad that I know
Him and that I have learned to serve and worship Him in
and out of season. I am so grateful that I know His name,
but more importantly, I am blessed because He knows my
name. He created you and me with a plan according to
Jeremiah 29:11.

The train ride never seemed so short since I was actually
doing more than sleeping, yapping on the phone, texting
or talking. I can do all that later because one thing about
God is that although He has the power to do all things,
He still flows in seasons. You have to grab the opportunity
when it comes. You may or may not get that chance again
or you may have to sit on the bench and watch from the
sidelines with a disagreeable taste in your mouth as someone else does what you were asked to do. The day that I sat
on that train and began writing my story, I was grateful that
I was no longer procrastinating. I heard the train conduc-

tor make the announcement, "HALTHORPE, NEXT STOP." It was disappointing to arrive at destination because I did not want to stop writing. However, I knew I had something to look forward to doing on the train and in my spare time.

Something to Think About: *With all the noise surrounding us, it can almost cause us to miss our season. Are you maximizing your time wisely? What are you doing in your quiet, still moments? God wants to speak with you. I encourage you to be still and know that He is God. He is faithful. What did He reveal to you?*

Journal Entry: Book Expo

"When Elizabeth heard Mary's greeting, the baby leaped in her womb, and Elizabeth was filled with the Holy Spirit." (Luke 1:41)

Annual for some, but 2012 was my first time experiencing the African American Authors Expo at the Crowne Plaza Hotel in Timonium, Maryland. Wow! A part of my writing journey had begun. It felt good meeting, greeting, and listening to several authors who had just written their first book. Also, I marveled as I looked at the different professional book displays. Story and pitch lines were causing my new "writing baby" to kick in my belly.

Ms. Tanya, Ms. Adams, & Ladybug Productions, just to name a few, were among the over fifty authors in attendance. I was only able to speak to a few, but a couple of them were divine connections. My spirit leaped like a frog the way I can imagine Elizabeth's and Mary's babies kicked in the Bible. When I met Ladybug Productions, I was able to connect her to my cousin, Derrick Lee Mitchell, who is an author and illustrator. She had been looking for an illustrator so hopefully they will be able to partner up.

Mr. Kool-Aid would have been unemployed because I was cheesing and smiling so hard I could have taken his job. I was happy and excited because I was aligning myself towards one of my God-given dreams. In the summer of 1996, I received a prophecy about me writing books. Months earlier, I had rededicated my life to Christ as my oldest brother was on his death bed. My brother's death brought forth my spiritual life. It was during that time that I realized I needed God in my life for real.

Although I was raised in the church as a child, I had begun my spiritual walk of faith in 1996 and I believed God for the impossible. I was witnessing to everyone in hopes to lead them to Christ. I wanted everybody to be saved and for them to experience amazing encounters like me. I prayed for just about anyone, including my enemies. Since I had received so much grace and mercy, I wanted to introduce everyone to Christ as their Savior. Now I understand that the way I was responding was the role of an evangelist. I was not looking for a title but just wanted people to be saved and restored. I share that same conviction today.

Now years and years later, the prophecy is finally starting to come into existence. The expo took place in August 2012 and it seemed like immediately after the event I starting writing. It was amazing how God gave me so many ideas and how the majority of my book was written on my way to work on the commuter train. But then, there was a break and I stopped writing regularly and I would only write periodically. Please note: although I stopped writing, likely due to a combination of reasons God was always reminding me to get back to the task. He used many ways to get my attention and get me back into writing my story-through sermons, intimate prayer time, mere prophecies, and even through conversations with people I knew personally who had written their first books.

During those times, I wish I could say that I always picked up the pen, (well due to technology, the tablet) and began writing. However, it did not always work out that way, but I did gain encouragement that I could begin writing my books. Then there were times I would have to repent for procrastinating.

Weeks later, I was able to talk to another good friend and let her know that I attended the Book Expo. I told my friend that I was claiming that I would be there as a new author promoting my books next year. Although it had not yet manifested, I was still believing God for it. This friend calls me "Hallelujah Praiser" because of my radical praise, and I always find joy and laughter when we talk. She and I often have unrehearsed God-appointed conversations which leads us to exalting and praising God when His presence shows us. It is always refreshing and encouraging that our labor is not in vain. Also, God will give us a glimpse of his promise which in turn motivates us to not give up but to keep waiting on Him. I learned in one of our conversations that she had been writing her book as well which was a pleasant surprise.

On the next page is a Prayer Affirmation to help you develop 3 steps towards a goal/dream you have. After you fill in the blank with your goal, give it a date to have that step completed. Read the Prayer Affirmation out loud as a declaration to what you believe God will help you do.

Something to Think About: *Have you ever received a prophecy and your current situation did not match what was spoken? How did you learn to come in agreement with God? Is there an assignment God has called you to fulfill but you are having a hard believing it will come to pass? What are three steps you can take to help you fulfil on the assignment?*

PRAYER AFFIRMATION:

DEAR LORD, I WANT TO THANK YOU FOR BEING A SOVEREIGN AND HOLY GOD. GOD, I THANK YOU THAT YOU CREATED ME WITH A PURPOSE. YOU SAID, IF I DELIGHT MYSELF IN YOU, THEN YOU WOULD GIVE ME MY HEARTS DESIRES (PSALM 37:4). LORD I WANT TO COMPLETE (FILL IN THE BLANK) WHICH YOU CALLED ME TO DO. HELP ME IN MY UNBELIEF. I DECLARE TODAY THAT I WILL WORK TOWARDS MY GOALS. I WILL ACTIVATE MY FAITH BY FOLLOWING THE 3 STEPS WRITTEN BELOW:

1. _____

   DUE DATE _____

2. _____

   DUE DATE _____

3. _____

   DUE DATE _____

I BELIEVE THAT YOU WILL CONNECT ME WITH THE RESOURCES AND THE PEOPLE TO ASSIST ME WITH THE TASK AT HAND. I AM STANDING ON YOUR WORD THAT «I CAN DO ALL THINGS THROUGH CHRIST JESUS WHO STRENGTHENS ME» (PHILIPPIANS 4:13). I CLAIM IT AND BELIEVE IT. IN JESUS' NAME I PRAY. AMEN! AMEN! AMEN!!!

Journal Entry: Stepping Out

" But the boat was now in the midst of the sea
distressed by the waves; for the wind was con-
trary…. And he said, 'Come'. And Peter went down
from the boat, and walked upon the waters to come
to Jesus" (Matthew 14:24, 29)

One foot proceeds forward then the other foot follows almost automatically. You are taking the steps you need to pursue your dreams and goals. You are beating the odds by daring to step out and move forward. Who said that you had to do it like Johnny, Tracy, Tasha, or Nicole? God created you to be fearfully and wonderfully made. You are created in His image to do great and mighty things through His strength. You are an individual with ideas from the Lord who has infinite wisdom and unlimited re-sources.

Dare to take God at His word by trusting Him "with all your heart and lean not unto your own understanding; in all your ways acknowledge him and he will direct your path" (Proverbs 3:5-6). When we trust God, He opens up doors for us. God loves when we activate (walk into know-ing) our faith and trust Him and His Word. He shall per-form it. According to Isaiah 55, God's Word will not return void but accomplish what it was sent out to do. Faith can move mountains.

POWER OF INFLUENCE

When you do your God-given purpose it helps others to get aligned in their purpose and to get their needs met. It's amazing how nature works. People cross your path for various reasons and seasons to help you directly or indirectly. I am even bold enough to say that even your enemies can help you, even when it is not their intentions. The Bible states that God will make even your enemies to be at peace with you and will make your enemies your footstool. Footstools allow you to go higher than you were at your last level. You rise up! Whether it is great or small, you still move upward.

Who you are can make such a difference in the lives of those you come in contact with. As I am writing this book, I am fulfilling one of many assignments which means that I have aligned myself with God's will. As my pastor, Dr. Karen Bethea, often states, "God is so economical." He never asks us to do something just to be a blessing to ourselves, but rather to reach many people. With that being said, I was talking with my friend who is about to start her business. She and I have had discussions over the past year but now she is moving towards her dream even more. We've bounced ideas around and it was like there was an ignition inside of each of us. I shared with her some of the knowledge I had gained from starting a dance studio business. Our past experiences shared a purpose and now added more definition to our lives, regardless of any bitter and temporary moments that may have occurred. Now we each have gained insight. It brings to mind the scripture, Romans 8:28 which states that all things work together for the good of them that love the Lord. Which means that in your journey of faith, you will experience joyful and painful moments in life. However, with God on your side, you will be shielded and protected and He will turn your pain into purpose. Also, he turns your pain into purpose.

As my friend and I continued to talk, I told her that I started writing this book and I have several more books to write. She was pleasantly surprised. We were grateful how God was speaking to us in our dreams and confirming what He told us to do through different people. We were meeting strangers who had similar ideas to help us cultivate this new place in our lives. Wisdom, knowledge and understanding were flowing like milk and honey. We made a pact to encourage each other until we push the babies out at full term. We recognized that this is a mountain top experience that we do not want to end.

Something to Think About: *During your last mountain top experience with God, what did He tell you to Step Out to do? What is holding you back? You can do it*

Journal Entry: Wait on Him!

"I waited patiently for the Lord; he turned to me and heard my cry." (Psalms 40:1)

Years ago, while a good friend of mine was visiting, we were talking, catching up, encouraging each other, being silly and radical for Jesus. We became so hyped thinking about His goodness that we created a hip-hop club song, "Wait on Him Psalms 40." Our song was based on the scriptures, "They that wait upon the Lord, He shall renew their strength." We called my other friend and she chimed in even over the phone while we beat my table and beatboxed with our mouths. While it was all in fun, as we kept reflecting on God's goodness, we thought about those times when we waited on Him and He showed up and showed out. With great anticipation of what our future would be according to His promises, our faith was boiling over which lead to a Glory Break! Wait on Him- Psalms 40!

Something to Think About: *It pays to Wait on God but make sure you are activating your Faith in the Meanwhile stage. Faith without works is dead.*

Journal Entry: What is Success to You?

"…Jehoshaphat stood and said, Hear me, O Judah, and you inhabitants of Jerusalem; Believe in the LORD your God, and you shall be established; believe His prophets, and you shall prosper."
(2 Chronicles 20:20)

One evening, as I was watching a church service on television, a preacher delivered a great sermon that really touched my soul. The premise of the sermon was: believe God and you will succeed.

Some of the key points that his sermon touched on were:

You must have a Word from God. What are your gifts; what are you good at? Confirmation for me was others around me were writing and publishing their books and I needed to finish my book. One word from God can and has changed my life.

You must have a testimony. Sometimes, the greater your trials, the stronger the encouragement, and eventually the greater you will exalt God for His glory. The Best is yet to come. God is my Source.

Don't give up. The power of perseverance. Despise not small beginnings. The dream will grow. Habakkuk 4

Know that God's delays are not God's denials. God is not limited by time. Nothing worth getting is gained overnight unless it is by His Grace. However, be not weary in well doing. Romans 8:28

<u>"No" is not always a bad response.</u> It protects us. Not now. God has something better. No progress without process. Do my best and leave the rest to God. Proverbs 3:5-7. II

<u>Go forward in the power and might of the Spirit.</u> David depended on God and beat Goliath. Obey God and develop learned obedience.

Thank you Jesus. I needed this Word. My spirit felt heavy and a little defeated because my dream of my home and mate were not manifesting as 2013 approached. Lord thank you Jesus for your Favor. When one of my friends stated that he wanted Anointed Touch Dance Ministry (ATDM), my dance organization to dance for him I became so excited. Also, he wanted to donate a toy to the shelter where ATDM serves.

Each December ATDM partners with sponsors to have a toy and food drive at a local shelter. My friend Shirl and I started the toy drive between 2006 and 2007. ATDM continued for about 9 years. It was amazing how God provided and expanded our resources. When we first started out, we only had 10 toys to give away because we wanted to use what we had. As the years progressed, other sponsors saw how Anointed Touch was serving the community and they began to support us. The children in the shelters began receiving 3 to 4 toys each along with hats, gloves, coats and food. The parents even received some gifts, too. I share this story because it demonstrates how you should not despise small beginnings. Continue to be consistent with pursuing your dream and God will send your additional support.

What is Success to You? is such a thought-provoking question. These experiences, along with several others, have helped to bring this book into existence. The sermons were so significant that I had to include some of the actual notes typed as well as my response to the message. In the upcoming, Workbook version of Stepping Out on Faith Dare to Dream: Journal of Faith, I actually write what I think success is. Although I did not include all the sermons, know that as I continued to put this book off, God reminded me daily to complete it. I truly know that for Him to press on me so much, that I needed to write it, just as Jesus needed to go to Samaria because He had a purpose to fulfill and he had to change the Samaritan woman's life forever. God is using this book to help change your life as He changed my life.

He saved me from a life of sin, low self-esteem, legalistic thinking, self-righteousness, judgment, nervousness, and anxiety to a life which is beautiful, inside and out, Confident, Encouraging, Saved, Energetic, and Excited. And now I am a Radical Woman of Faith who shares the Good News wherever I go.

Something to Think About: *Have you ever felt like your dream was delayed and would never come to pass? What do you consider as successful? How close are you to obtaining your success? I pray that this book has inspired you and may God be glorified. Truly delighting in Him, he will give you your heart's desires. Do not believe the lies of the enemy. With God, all things are possible. Much love and sincerest prayers are extended for your life to know that doing the Will of God provides the Greatest Success.*

Journal Entry: Shifting in your Anointing

"Trust in the LORD with all your heart, and lean not on your own understanding. In all your ways acknowledge Him, and He shall direct your paths."
(Proverb 3:5-6)

Am I really trusting God?

☐ What am I trusting Him for?

☐ Am I keeping God first?

Am I ready for change? Am I doing what God called and designed me to do? These are some of the very questions we may ponder when we prepare to shift. Shifting into your anointing requires separation, change, transition, uncomfortable moments, humility, trust and leaning on God. Separation: an act of moving, or being moved, apart. Synonym: disconnection. God may put people in our space for a short time, a season, if you will. But when that season is over and it is time to hear from Him, it's time to move from the crowd to be set apart for His use. Jesus was another great example of this. There was time that Jesus spent with for the disciples and the crowds, but it was a daily practice for Him to be separate from them to hear from God and to spend that quiet time with the Lord.

As you spend time with the Lord, it will ultimately bring about change on the inside and outside. In His presence, there is fullness of joy. He turns our mourning into dancing. He gives us beauty for ashes. As you change, a transition takes place. Your mind shifts, it takes off that old nature and puts on a new one- shifting from baseline to a higher level. As exciting as a transition can be, it is also often most uncomfortable because you are experiencing new things such as starting a new job, getting married, having a baby, returning to school, changing a career, losing a loved one, or relocating.

You cannot rely heavily on the past; you need to trust God to be your navigator. Your old methods for solving matters or problems will not be sufficient in your new season. You must readjust since you have outgrown that old place. You must become humbled as you walk in faith and trust God in this new place. God promises to guide us. As you progress through each phase and you look back over your life, you will see how God really has been directing your steps to Shifting You into Your Anointing.

Something to Think About: *What phase are you currently in? Can you recall a time in which God directed you to separate from a person, place or thing and you did not understand or agree at the time? However, as time progresses, it will all make sense and you will realize that you are obedient. It is time to Shift.*

Journal Entry: Leap & Go Forward

Let us not become weary in doing good, for at
the proper time we will reap a harvest if we do not
give up. (Galatians 6:9)

As you shift into your new season, you prepare to leap and go forward, walking into your new season with faith and seeing the fruits of your labor. One plants, one waters and God gives the increase. Some blessings do take time to manifest but you have to keep pressing knowing that if you don't faint you will reap the harvest. Please be aware: although God has promised you your dream, there will still be distractions along the journey trying to compete for your attention. You will need to be focused. Unfortunately, this was a challenge for me, which is why this book took four years instead of six months to a year.

It is amazing how pain or discomfort can either stop you in your tracks or push you into you purpose. I have experienced both on numerous occasions. Sometimes disagreements with loved ones forced me to go to my quiet place and find inner peace in the Lord. As I write this now, it feels so relaxing and soothing as I commute to work on the MARC train. {Selah, Selah, Selah} Thank you Lord that what the enemy means harm, You made it good. Let me tell you that when you are given an assignment by the Lord, He will make every provision for it even when it seems impossible to complete. God will provide. However, when the brook dries up and the chapter has come to a close, that is when it is time to seek God for the next location and assignment.

Have you ever felt stuck but you were too afraid to leap and go forward? The Bible says to not be afraid but to be encouraged because He is with us. Do not let fear keep you trapped in a particular situation when God wants to move you forward. If you remain in a season that needs to end, it becomes frustrating during the transition period. In addition, things start falling apart and not flowing because the grace of God had lifted for that season. Expect more turmoil if His grace for that task has ceased. However, if you obey God and Leap & Go Forward even afraid or nervous, God will not let you fall. Say "Yes" to him and then a peace will overtake you that you just can't imagine. Trust him to help your transition forward to that "new place".

Something to Think About: *You must know that although God gives you an assignment, you will still have distractions to attempt to draw your eyes in another direction. Please note that all distractions do not come as a negative person, place or thing. It may be that at that particular time you may have to decline an offer to hang out, talk on the phone, go to the additional service, and or not overcommit yourself. Are you willing to leap and go forward on your journey?*

Journal Entry: Roadrunner.... Beep Beep

"Martha, Martha," the Lord answered, "you are worried and upset about many things, but few things are needed—or indeed only one. Mary has chosen what is better, and it will not be taken away from her." (Luke 10:41-42)

Can you relate to any of the following expressions or thoughts below?

"Slow down and rest"

"It is time to hustle and bustle, Excuse me?"

("Can I get by you? I have somewhere to be!"

"This traffic is ridiculous." (Road Rage)

"I'm sorry, not now, I have to go."

"I have no time for personal devotion. I'm late!"

"Pray?? Who has a time for that?"

"CHOP CHOP Let's get it done!"

Those expressions and thoughts indicate there is a rush and there is no time to waste. However, it could be that you have overcommitted yourself; maybe you spread yourself too thin; or you did not take time to rest in God's presence in prayer. When we rest in His presence, He gives strategies and direction to complete the task given to you to help you be successful. When you were asked to sign up on that committee, maybe you should have declined since you assisted the last three times. Instead of you signing up, God may have wanted you to go visit a lonely family member to build their spirit. It is important to be turned into the voice of God and obey Him for new instructions. For instance, over the past three years, ideas and planning for the committee were coming without fail but this year it was a halt. You just could not figure out why you felt tired and frustrated while working on the committee. You think, 'Well I am doing a good deed, right?' However, you cannot do everything or be everywhere, especially since God was shifting you to do another task. It was out of habit and familiarity, you continued doing the same thing. During that time, you worked on that committee it was not productive or fruitful without God's approval.

This is where the Shifting into Your Anointing the Change phrase occurs. God did not tell you to take on that obligation which is why it is not working out right. It is then that you may need to, throw your hands up and ask God for help. A prayer as simple as, "Lord have mercy on me," can provide the calm that is needed in stressful times. It is a time to be humble. Then there are the moments when all you can do is shake your head and hope for another time to seek direction from God first.

In addition, listen to your body when it speaks: eat healthy, drink plenty of water, exercise, rest, and relax. If you abuse or neglect your body, it will begin to shut down on you. There were many times I became ill because I was a "Road Runner" and not able or bold enough to tell others "No." Therefore, I ended up with strong episodes of vertigo. During those times, my equilibrium was off which means I was not balanced and I required help from others.

Apostle Karen preached on the importance of being in the presence of God and obeying His voice, rather than man. She shared how certain seasons require that we steal away to know what God wants us to do. This sermon hit home especially when she mentioned that I needed to stop supporting my family so much. I was getting burned out and getting in the way of God. I had to learn to say "No" without feeling guilty. I was focused more on meeting the needs of my family than taking care of what God called me to do. I was doing more pouring out than getting replenished. At first, assisting my family was partly my assignment to help bring more unity. However, that season ended – the grace had been lifted for that task. What was meant to be a temporary assistance turned into over 3½ years. Prior to me helping my family, I was trying to purchase a home3½-year experience.

God told me that he was not going to release my home to me until I released my family to Him. I enjoyed helping out and being with my family but I was blocking my own blessings as well as theirs. I would watch the kids because it was something I desired. Thus, I would make plans around my niece and nephew's schedule. My friends had told me, "Peaches, you don't have children. You are free to do what you want." However, I was consumed in the role of "helper." It was not until I made the decision to take a stand and set boundaries that I was able to accomplish my own goals. Once I did, let go, God worked out those things and situations I was concerned about. God showed that He is our provider, not our job. I was looking with blurred glasses. God provided a new apartment for my sister and her family one week after I purchased my home. I had exhausted my resources because I am human however, God's resources can never be spread too thin.

Something to Think About: *Have you ever been so busy that time passed you by when God told you personally to just slow down for a minute?*

It is importance to learn how to set boundaries and learn to use your time wisely. Do not over-commit yourself just to receive the approval of man. Make sure you are doing what God called you to do.

In the Midst of the Race

Journal Entry: Eat the Fish, Spit Out the Bones

"God's will (for your life) is for you to be holy, so stay away from all sexual sin. Then each of you will control his own body and live in holiness and honor..." (1 Thessalonians 4:3-7)

The summer of 2012, I was taking a ride down on 95 South with a close friend. We were headed on our first cruise. It was interesting for us to learn more about one another. She is one of my best friends forever (BFFs) and we formerly met as neighbors five years prior to the trip. I've given her many names according to the myriad roles she plays in her community, on her job, at her church, in her family, and socially. We admonish and encourage each other to grow higher in our spiritual, professional, and personal lives. We extend our advice freely and can engage in humor at the same time.

Last year we were discussing a bestseller book on relationships by a well-renowned author. As views were exchanged, I told my friend that some of what the male author wrote had some truth to it and made sense. It was also noted that I did not agree with all of the advice and strategies the author expanded on because it went against the Word of God. I told my friend that I will "eat the fish and spit out the bones." She giggled when I explained what it meant and I laughed too, amazed that she had never heard that old saying. Who should get the credit for originating it? I have no idea and for the purpose of this book it doesn't matter. The expression means that although some good advice was given about how to maintain a good relationship or to recognize if you are even in one or not, the advice was not considered good if it went against the Word of God. The author endorsed the idea of "test driving" in a new relationship, or "trying to milk before purchasing the cow." In other words, he promoted premarital sex, which is strictly against the Word of God, according to 1 Corinthians 6:9-11. Thus, statements surrounding that theme were considered "fish bones" and were spit out. Just like one can choke and die physically from ingesting fish bones, one can die spiritually doing things that choke their spirit like adultery, fornication, and sexual pleasures outside of the sanctity of marriage between a man and woman. As much as I want to be happily married, and I won't compromise my faith to please my flesh. I have been there and done that. I share below how I yielded to my flesh.

I once focused on pleasing my flesh, but now that chapter is closed. I will not deny that I had some fun times in previous relationships. However, it was not fun to hear about my ex-boyfriend cheating constantly and it was not fun getting a sexually transmitted disease from him because he was never satisfied with me alone. As I became closer to God, I saw how I was selling my soul for a few moments of pleasure to someone who was not my husband. Although I was faithful in the relationship, and I wanted us to be exclusive, it was not the same as marriage. He denied sleeping around but it was evident he was seeing other females. Some of those females were my friends and family but I was never the type to argue or fight. I was angry and I was sad, but when I broke up with him, it was only temporary. I knew he was not good for me but my low self-esteem wanted the attention and to fill loved. Also, I was trying to fill a void that only God could fill. Our continued sexual connection created in me a negative soul tie that I thought I could not break. All my family and friends told me to stop dealing with him. However, it took me rededicating my life back to God in college and moving away to begin my new life. I enrolled into graduate school for Social Work in Baltimore to break the toxic cycle.

For once, my pride was what helped me to not return to that unhealthy relationship and the long distance. I decided to begin a road of celibacy which was a process of mental warfare. It was a challenge, but by God's grace, I managed to remain abstinent for three and a half years until I married to my late husband Matthew Kenney. It was amazing because I never thought I could live without having sex.

Watching Christian videos about sexual impurities and participating in a Youth Impact Conference in Atlanta opened my eyes even more about fornication and how it does not please God. I found this out the hard way. I learned since the Holy Spirit resides in me now it does not want unwelcomed spirits from anyone who is not my husband. Also, I learned at the conference that each time I had premarital sex, I was raping the Holy Spirit. By definition, rape is of coerced force, placed on someone without their permission. And surely the Holy Spirit did not ask to be violated nor did it deserve it.

So much time had passed after the death of my husband, and one could not have told me that I would succumb to my flesh since my relationship with the Lord was stronger. I was setting the bar high and I was the example and role model for friends to stand strong. However, after eight years of celibacy and yielding to God, I created a written vision of what I desired my Christian mate to look like. My mind was made up that I would not be having anymore premarital sex until I had Mr. RIGHT'S last name. I normally wouldn't even waste my time talking to guys especially if I could tell that were not trying to live holy. However, in 2010 I met a counterfeit and unfortunately I yielded to my flesh, as much as I attempted to resist. I became weary in my well doing. I became tired of waiting years without a mate.

Please be advised, if you play with fire, you will get burned. It started out with just holding hands, showing affection, talking on the phone, a light kiss, a hug, then touch which eventually progressed to being completely intimate and having sex. How did I fall for this trap again after 8 years? That was a challenging year for me. I'm glad I lived to tell the story and I was not thrown into the Lake of Fire for brief moments of pleasure. I truly found myself in a place I didn't want to be spiritually, even though my flesh yearned for it. I thank my dear friend, who rebuked me at that level of accountability and helped me to be free and bring forth my deliverance. I had to repent and God restored and renewed me. It has been several years now I am waiting on God's Best. God is truly my keeper.

Taking a stand like that sounds strong but it was sometimes painful and lonely, especially when I saw other couples saved - or not - yielding to their flesh. My fleshly thoughts at times would try to drift back but I had to rebuke it and declare my stand by faith. In addition, I have to be careful of what I watch and listen to in order to reduce temptation. I would cry out to God asking, "Lord, how much longer will I have to wait before I am discovered again?" I was a young woman full of life and promise, when I lost my husband tragically, to violence in the streets of Baltimore in 2001.

During that season, I learned God in a whole new way. I am resting in his arms and declaring his goodness. Again, I praise God for redemption and restoration daily. He has turned my mourning into dancing. In choosing who your friends will be, make sure they will hold you accountable and push you into your purpose.

Something to Think About: *Do you have anyone in your circle of influence that can hold you accountable to the Word and Will of God? Who in your circle motivates you to live out your God-given Destiny? If you can't answer these questions, pray and ask God for people like that. He will do it. Iron sharpens iron.*

Journal Entry: Don't Settle

"Delight yourself in the Lord, and he will give you the desires of your heart." (Psalm 37:4)

One morning I posted on Facebook that when we are impatient we tend to miss the 1st place prize. Thus, we settle for being in 2nd or 3rd place, when God designed us to be champions. Being impatient is a temporary fix for a problem to fill a need or desire. Delayed gratification, however, means one was patient and waited on God then you will receive his BEST. God displayed that he gave His best when He offered His son, Jesus to die for us.

I had to let go of the "woe is me" and the "impoverished" mindsets. I am a child of God -- A king's kid --Royalty. I would encourage myself, "You deserve to receive God's best rather than settling for average. I had to let go of the idea that I was not good enough. When I thought like that, I found myself settling for less than I what I deserved. I am precious in the sight of God. God renewing my mind and upgrading who I am in the kingdom. God promised to give us our hearts desires if we delight in Him.

I deserve the Best. You deserve the Best. Thus, do not accept less than your worth. Realize that your destiny and purpose is at stake when you compromise and settle. We have one life to live, so make it the best life ever.

Something to Think About: *Are you settling for less than you deserve? Are you trying to make a temporary fix into a permanent situation? Remember, our decisions today will play out in our future circumstances. Choose wisely.*

Journal Entry: Freshness of a New Opportunity

"And I will restore to you the years that the locust hath eaten, the canker-worm, and the caterpillar, and the palmer-worm, my great army which I sent among you." (Joel 2:25)

"Remember ye not the former things, neither consider the things of old. Behold, I will do a new thing; now shall it spring forth; shall ye not know it? I will even make a way in the wilderness, and the rivers in the desert. (Isaiah 43:18-19)

Smiles. A flicker in my heart is brightened as I reflect. Times have finally changed for the better and that long awaited desire is close approaching. Long suffering, meanwhile, the sun seems to sparkle more even when there is overcast. God is truly faithful to do exceedingly, abundantly, above all we can ask or think. Have you figured it out? I met someone who fits the vision of the type of man I would want to marry. It is still very low key and moving at a slow pace. Now we are just new friends and there have not been any dates. I have been encouraged by it being a possibility. Also, it is a blessing to see there are still rams in the bush. We do have a few single, straight, Christian men without any children desiring marriage. I am not jumping the broom, but it lets me know that God is able and I do not have to settle.

Truly, I been waiting to be in a healthy relationship for a longtime. I tried to get it in Godly and not-so- Godly ways. I shared how after abstaining for 8 years, I got weary in waiting and I settled for a county Bozo. Then I met several men who appeared to be a good match for me. However, their spiritual commitment to Christ was missing in their lives. They were still "searching" as they say. I only talked to few other Christian men. Each of them told me that I was nice, intelligent, "blah, blah, and blah…." However, they were either not ready to be in a relationship or they were seeing other women. I was their Plan B or Plan C which bothered my psyche at times. I questioned, What was wrong with me? Why was I not the apple of anyone's eye? Time would only tell if the possibility would turn into a reality. Tick tock, tick tock, tick tock. Meanwhile let us just be friends. Even if the friendship does not progress to a relationship, the gentlemen was like a prototype of man I visualized. It gave me hope that God had not forgotten me and I could receive his best.

Prototypes or models are examples of what a person can look forward to in the future. If you are leasing an apartment, the leasing agent shows you the model apartment with furniture, pictures, and fixtures. This is not yours but it helps you to visualize your own. Your apartment will actually be empty with fresh carpet, but now you can imagine how to set up your place as you would like to have it. If you obey Him, you will be shown a picture of what your life can be just like being shown a model apartment.

Something to Think About: *Have you written a vision for what you are desiring? Has God shown you a glimpse of what he has in store for you? It is time Step forward and believe it can happen. God has something NEW in store for your Life. Receive it today.*

Journal Entry: No Energy Drink

"I can do all things through Christ who strengthens me."
(Philippians 4:13)

No Energy drink, no box of Wheaties, no Spanish fly and no steroids. Limited human strength. God's super added to our natural strength always works.

In preparation to minister in dance, take a long drive or after a long day, my friend and I would drink an energy drink to boost our energy and keep us more alert for the hours ahead. There would be a momentary increase in our energy level. However, there are times I have gone without any energy drink and I had to rely on God's Supernatural strength. I would be extremely tired from working, serving in ministry, or just completing everyday tasks and I would pray to God to please restore me.

According to Psalm 23, He does restore our souls and allows us to rest in Him. God would sometimes provide me with so much strength and joy that it would be contagious to those I encounter. My exhausted body and mind would feel renewed to complete the task at hand. It's been revealed to me that when I dance in the Holy Spirit, even when tired, my energy is sustained. But once the dance was done and the assignment is complete, His grace lifts. Therefore, I am left to realize that God had truly shown up and worked through me because then my energy would almost be depleted. God made the provision as long it was needed.

Something to Think About: *What shortcuts have you been taking to try to resolve a problem that appeared too overwhelming for you? Do you have days when your energy fills depleted? Try praying to ask God for assistance in the matter and listen to his strategies.*

Journal Entry: Cedar Drive Promise

"And Jehovah answered me, and said, Write the vision and make it plain upon tablets, that he may run that readeth it. For the vision is yet for an appointed time and it hasteth toward the end, and shall not lie: though it tarry, wait for it, because it will surely come, it will not delay. (Habakkuk2: 2-4)

In August of 2001, I received a prophecy that God was going to bless me with a particular home which had matched my written vision. Days after I received the prophecy, I met with a realtor and he showed me a home that was on Cedar Drive. I prayed for that home and I believed for years that was going to be my home one day. I used to think that seeing the word very often that was my confirmation and sign that home would be my future residence. However, I became frustrated that the prophecy did not come to pass and starting losing hope.

For example, years after the prophecy, I recall seeing a street called Cedar in Washington, DC as I was driving in the field one day. Then, I saw Cedar Circle driving home and I passed apartments called, Cedar Garden and Towers. I did not get as excited as I used to when I saw the word cedar. I purposely did not pay attention to it. I had been waiting to buy a home on Cedar Drive. I thought, "Thank you Lord for I believe you would bless me with the home but it may not be on Cedar Drive. I admitted I was getting tired of seeing the word, cedar. It reminded me of something I been praying and waiting for a long time and I was wondering what I'm was supposed to do to obtain the home on Cedar Drive. Lord, it's not like it is just going to come to my doorstep. I would need your favor and finances. Based on the prophecy, the home was waiting on me between Woodlawn and Randallstown in Lochearn. The home on Cedar Drive fit the description of my vision and the location. I thought, "Lord you lead me to the house on Cedar Drive and there it had everything that was written in my vision from August 2001 until October 2012. Lord, you said be not weary in well doing because in due time I will reap if I faint not. Lord what do I need to do? Lord I believe but help my unbelief. It is time for me to move out this apartment into my home. I kept being denied on home loans and I know that you have not had me wait this long to not come out on top with a powerful testimony."

I prayed I knew that everything works in my favor and that I will be house rich, with a fully furnished home and financially overflowing including, paying my student loans, and my mortgage will be significantly less than my rent. My faith had been tested for at least eleven years but I still believed that God was more than able. You told Pastor Karen that a warehouse was her church and you blessed her with the church. Lord it was not long afterwards that you showed me my vision but this promise has not manifested. What am I doing wrong? What do I need to do? God hear my cry? This mold invested apartment is negatively affecting my lungs.

Four years in this mold-infested apartment has created health problems. Upper respiratory problems and wheezing, even yesterday I was having a hard time breathing and feeling fatigued. Lord I am hurting some and I am tired with anger but yet I trust and will praise your name. You are worthy of the praise you are my God and my help in the time of trouble. You are my strong tower. There is nothing too hard for you. I know that you are going to bless me despite the wait.

I did not get the home on Cedar however, God did still bless me with my first home as Single, African American woman. My home was similar to the house he revealed to me in August of 2001, but a smaller version. God really provides us what we really need and can handle. The house he showed me I would need a driving lawn mower to maintain the grass, and I am just not ready for that. However, I believe my Boaz will handle those outside duties. With that being said, God was still faithful to his promise and I can handle this home. If I am faithful with a little, then God will make me ruler over many. The other home that I had my mind set on was too BIG for me to be able to manage properly. It would have been more damage than good. This is an upgrade from my two-bedroom apartment that I had for years so I am grateful. This will be my investment home because Greater is coming.

I thank God I am now a proud home owner of a three-bedroom brick townhouse, 2 levels and a basement with a fireplace, laundry room, 2 full baths, plenty of storage, parking pad, garage, front porch, back patio, front yard, stainless steel appliances, and granite countertops in backsplash in the kitchen, & more. This home was setting waiting for me and it had been renovated. Just to share and encourage you with a brief testimony about this home.

On May 21, 2014, the spirit of God dropped in my spirit for me to resubmit my application for my home buyer's program that day. Please note God had been telling me to reapply for my home loans for the past couple of years but my faith did get tired of being denied but I never gave up completely. On that day, I felt such a heaviness to obey God and submit my packet. Part of my reservations came from me completing the budget forms and seeing that I was in the red zone meaning it would appear that I could not afford a home. Although I was paying my tithes and offerings faithfully, I did not want the Home Buying Counselor or Loan Officer tell me that I could not get my home after I knew that I was overdue for my home. I had to step out on faith.

After my "Faith Facts" bible study class I wanted to speak to my instructor to share how God confirmed about my home and me writing books. However, I truly believe God allowed her to be engulfed into a conversation in order for me to leave to go to Staples and drop off my application at the housing program. It was after 9:30pm and I was rushing down I695 praying, praising, & listening to the preached Word on a cd. It was Bishop Kenneth Robinson who spoke at our church anniversary and God used him to say that we must be obedient to God. Also, he stated that there are some blessings that God has in store for us but he is waiting for us to Show up and God will have the right people in place to assist you. My faith tank was overflowing then a reality set in that it was 10:00pm at night and the housing program did not have a mail slot or drop box. Business hours ended at 5pm but I kept reminding God that I was being obedient to what he said. It was not a surprise that the doors were locked however I saw a light on. I knocked on the glass door and a woman came to the door who was a custodian. I told her that I knew that she was not supposed to do this but would she please put my application on the desk. The lady said with a smile that she would. All I could do was shout and worship God because my obedience lead to my on time blessing. God had orchestrated that custodian to be working late that night to assist me.

A few weeks after I submitted my packet, I had my one to one session and met my new Christian realtor. I reapplied for my mortgage loan and was approved. On June 21, 2014, I went looking at homes. My home was the second home that I saw and I feel in love with it. My sister, niece and nephew went with me despite of me having a migraine headache. My sister asked "How long had this house been on the market?" My realtor said that it had been on since May 22, 2014. At the moment, the light bulb did not go off on the significance of that date. However, on June 28, 2014 Anointed Touch Dance Ministry we had the opportunity to minister dance in my hometown in Salisbury, Maryland. After we ministered the spirit of God ministered to my spirit and he told me that by me listening to him on May 21, 2014 that I was finally buying my home. My house went on the market the very next day after I submitted my application packet to the housing program. I put a bid on the house on June 23, 2014 and it was accepted by June 28, 2014 and I received my keys on September 23, 2014 and I moved in October 2014. Won't HE DO IT??!!

The cost of the home was dropped by $9,000 and God has given me favor with my neighbors. By His grace, my home was move-in ready and fully furnished within a month of me moving in without me compromising my Christian values or morals. This is my first home not my last and it has been dedicated back to God.

Something to Think About: *Obedience to God often can go against the norms because it is normally an act of faith. Naturally it would not have made sense for me to drive to a business that was closed to submit my application, however God said it and He had the custodian right there to help me. The rest is history. Do what God says...*

Home Stretch: The Finish Line

Spa Birthing to Fruition

And she, being with child cried, travailing in
birth, and pained to be delivered. (Revelation 12:2)

<small>JOURNEY ENTRY SPA BIRTHING TO FRUITION</small>

Well in the Beginning of the Book I speak about the Spa Retreat and towards the end I am ending with it. It can go without saying that my experiences at the Spa Retreat had a significant impact on my spiritual & natural life. I shared past and present challenges and victorious that have occurred in my life. All along the birthing of the book, Stepping Out on Faith Dare to Dream: Journal of Faith went from a prophecy to an actual book. The last few chapters get more intense. My faith level increases and I learn to hear and obey the voice of God. God proves Himself and more prayers are answered. Keep on reading and be encouraged.

Now I must go with the theme of the Spa Retreat 2015 "This Girl Is on Fire" hosted by my Apostle Dr. Karen S. Bethea. This conference put me directly on the delivery table with my midwives to finally push out this book. I saw a natural shifting from dance to writing. I was initially sitting with the dancers but I was drawn to sit by another published author who has been admonishing me to write since I told her. This time the Holy Spirit spoke directly to me that I had to set aside the next two weeks and focus on this book. Trust me there were sacrifices to be made especially for a social butterfly like me. I communicated with my dear friends to let them know that I would be on a sabbatical for the next few weeks with limited communication with them. Well if you are reading this sentence it means that I PUSHED this book out.

Something to Think About: *In order to give birth, it is a sign of expectancy that brings lots of joy & excitement. However, birthing involves painful contractions that are necessary for the baby to be released. Don't Quit! The pain you are feeling is only labor pains pushing you into your Destiny. That was the title of my sermonette in leadership class in 2007. With that said, what is paining you so bad that it is crying to be completed?*

Journal Entry: No Limits Flying High in Arizona

"The earth's is the Lord's and the fullness thereof and all that is in it. (Psalms 24:1) But they who wait for the Lord shall renew their strength; they shall mount up with wings like eagles; they shall run and not be weary; they shall walk and not faint."
(Isaiah 40:31)

SUN VALLEY, ARIZONA

A good man's steps are ordered by the Lord.

It is the end of May 2015 and it is like my own memorial week due to the lovely memories I have experienced in Arizona. God's timing is beyond amazing and perfected. Traveling to Arizona, it was my first time in this state but my third time on the west coast. I had to visit a facility for business but it was such a lovely time. It did not feel like I was working. I met some nice people who were pleasant. I was able to meet a miracle baby who was born premature weighing only 1 pound. Looking at this chubby beautiful blue eyed precious bundle of joy, it would have not been known. Well I had the pleasure to meet her mother and grandmother as well. When they shared the baby's biblical name and her story I sensed in my spirit a divine connection. My spirit instantly went in prayer mode but I asked if I could pray for the baby. They wholeheartedly welcomed the prayer and gave thanks to God. With all of us being Believers, we affirmed each other and gave God praise. I read the Word for the day from Joel Osteen talked about God's favor and how He would bless our paths to cross the right people. It was a summary of this time in Arizona.

This miracle baby was told that she would not make it and that she would be delayed. Well we did not and had not accepted that report; instead we believed the report of the Lord. We declared healing and a uniquely advanced life and that she will serve the Lord, even at an early age. The grandmother was a little teary eyed and we all embraced and celebrated how God has His people over this whole world. We agreed that it is a small world after all. The mother actually taught me how to ride a horse. It was over 10 years ago when I last rode. She was a great teacher. It was funny, she looked like one of my friends in Baltimore.

In preparation for writing while in Arizona, I looked up Christian authors that I knew in Baltimore and I reached out to them. They responded and we have scheduled to speak to discuss my project. Also I asked my Pastor to add something in my book and she agreed. God is lining it all up. Amen I'm speaking to the atmosphere. I will have several book signings including for SOOF. I am believing God that I can do it at my church and other events in Jesus' name.

It is Thursday the day of my departure from Arizona but I am thinking of reasons to stay behind however I must head back to Baltimore. This trip served a lot of purposes in the natural as well as in the spiritual realm. There was even a delay with my pick-up time from the hotel yet it served as a purpose. God's hand was on in the mix. The original driver who picked me up from the airport when I arrived in Phoenix was able to drop me off. He was so kind and I told him that I would consider relocating to Arizona. He mentioned his church and how his pastor got delivered from the streets and gangs but he is giving back to the community.

That trip/experience was nothing BUT the grace of God. I was in the right place, being driven by the right person with the right information. The delay was nothing more than a setup by God to show me something different.

Something to Talk About: *Have you ever gone some place different but once you arrived, you had a unique godly encounter? Share how you noticed God ordering your steps to be at that very place.*

Journal Entry Instructions – SEEK HIM

I will instruct you and teach you in the way you should go; I will counsel you with my loving eye on you (Psalms 32:8)

Instructions, seek him while he may be found He will teach and guide you.

Step 1, Step 2, 1st, 2nd, 3rd and so forth are the ways we learned how to do things in the proper order. God is of impeccable order and the opposite of confusion. The Bible says to do all things in decency and in order. When we seek God's face He reveals hidden mysteries and he makes the foolish things wise. He provides strategies, creativity, and organization (I require extra grace in this area but one day I will be walking it out completely). He will make a HUGE project seem almost effortless when you obey His instructions step by step.

Now realistically I am aware that our human nature has the tendency to go against the grain and appease our flesh instead of following God's directions properly. As much as I love God with my saved, sold-out to Christ, and sanctified self, I do not always obey immediately when God speaks and gives me direction. I will say that most of the time I try but I miss the mark or I don't feel like doing what He is asking because I don't understand, I don't want to pay the price, I am being lazy, and, it looks too overwhelming. But God, as mentioned earlier, is faithful, merciful, and gracious towards us. He does not give us what we deserve. "THANK YOU, JESUS! THANK YOU FOR THE BLOOD OF JESUS! GLORY TO GOD!" < ·Glory Break! ·>.

There is hope for you if you missed the mark if you confess your sins, God is faithful and just to forgive us and cleanse us from all righteousness I John 1:9. Don't condemn yourself but rather use that uncomfortable feeling to push you to do better in obedience.

Something to Think About: *If you abide by God's Word in putting Him first according to Matthew 6:33, then he will provide what you stand in need of. So to complete your project, what do you need?*

Journal Entry I Believe God

"Have faith that you will receive whatever you ask
for in prayer." (Matthew 21:22)

Lord, I thank you for my rest, healing, and drawing me closer to you. Thank you for urging me to go forth as the Evangelist you called me to be. I cannot sit any longer. I plan to take some more spiritual leadership classes and get better at studying your Word. Lord you have given me a compassion for lost souls; to encourage them to return back to you. Most times it does not matter where I am, you will have me praying for someone to lead them back to you and then invite them church. Although, they may not come initially, I know that our encounter was God ordained and a seed of hope has been planted. As we pray God reveals what to pray for and once we are done the person confirms that was the area in which they needed prayer in.

I am glad I have been listening more to His voice when He says to witness or pray for others; but it is time for me to step out and go to the next level in ministry. I am eternally grateful for Anointed Touch Dance Ministry under the direction of Shirl Parnell. This ministry has been a training ground for me over the past twelve years. This ministry did not just teach dance but we actually witness to children, men, women, the broken hearted and lead others through Christ as we did outreach in the city of Baltimore. The motto for the ministry is "Change your Life & Come to Christ". We go throughout the streets of Baltimore and feed the homeless, minister at shelters, nursing homes, and in the market place. We have watched God change so many people's lives and turn them in new directions. It is a pleasure to share God's Word to others. God is so wonderful and He does not want any of us to perish.

I made some prayer declarations to the Lord by faith. I would usually start by thanking Him and I would speak into the atmosphere what I believe He would manifest. Please know that God is not a Santa Clause or genie that he grants wishes. God tells us to seek his kingdom and his righteousness and all things will be added to us. I thank you for my federal position and financial increase when it was time for me to return to Baltimore, Maryland. Thank you for allowing me to meet Ms. Burnett at the Marc station and speak to her today about her job. She works for the company I am interested in working at as a Health Insurance Specialist who travels. Only 10 minutes from my new home 15 min the max fully furnished neat and clean. Nice furniture and decor, 3 to 4 bedrooms. Favor: NEW LUXURY truck light blue Lexus truck, BMW or Benz. I will have my home this year in a few days and my new promotion and federal job. I will enjoy my job and I will advance in leadership with confidence in the Lord. Thank you, Jesus.

Well, that was then. I want to testify that God did it and He truly blew my mind with these and other blessings. They have been overtaking me within the last few years. To God be the glory! If we delight ourselves in Him, He will give us the desires of our hearts. God answered this declaration. He blessed me with a timeshare in 2013, my first luxury vehicle (a blue BMW), with my 1st home in September 2014, in 2015 my family went on a cruise, 2016 he blessed me with my second luxury vehicle, (blue Mercedes SUV), a new laptop to write my books and more. He allowed me to keep both of my vehicles and to have low car payments. My sister and her family are borrowing the BMW temporarily until they can purchase their own car. God knows that he has my heart and all that I mentioned above means nothing without Jesus Christ being lord over my life. I truly would rather have Him than silver and gold. Not only did God bless me with material blessings, he blessed me spiritually. He has increased the following: my faith, peace, joy, confidence, Holy Ghost boldness, ability to hear His voice, obedience, prayer life, ability to encourage and pray for others in their time of need, leadership skills, and witness.

Now those blessings did not happen overnight but I held on in faith for years believing that God would do it despite any setbacks or denials that came along the way. I learned to call those things which are not as though they were by faith.

Something to Think About: *What are you believing God for? SPEAK INTO THE ATMOSPHERE!!!*

Journal Entry: It's Not Over

"And there went out a champion out of the camp of the Philistines, named Goliath, of Gath, whose height was six cubits and a span." (I Sam 17:4)

Most people know the story of David & the giant Goliath. David was the smallest and youngest of his siblings yet he conquered Goliath despite his size and obstacles. His older brothers were fearful of Goliath but David seeing the challenge, he recognized with God being for him who could be against him. Thus, David saw the opposition as an opportunity. It seemed like it was going to be over for David - but God.

Think about the story of Lazarus who was actually dead. Death is normally final with no point of return. However, God did a miracle. After Lazarus was dead in the grave for 4 days, Jesus told Lazarus to come forth. You need to come forth as well.

Imagine this: as a child, you always had a childhood bully who would pick with you. However, after being tired of being taunted for a while, you finally fight back. Yet to your amazement you find the person was really afraid of you all along. Well that's what it's like for the enemy. He is seeking whom he can devour and blowing smoke screens hoping that you will run from him and not fulfill your God-given purpose. But sike devil the joke is on you. As we used to say when we know we won. "Na na na boo b oo! You can't get me." Yes it is an elementary "thang" to say but in essence it is the truth.

Lastly, let me share how God proves that it is not over

and that He is in control despite how it looks. I had been working in the District of Columbia for 4 years and my contract was coming to an end. I was not sure if my contract would be renewed or not since I was told that it may had reached its limit. So, I began applying for jobs and I had some good interviews. However, I was not selected as the candidate. Nevertheless, God had given me peace in my spirit even though my position may truly be ending anytime in the Spring.

I remember on June 10, 2016 I did a home visit and I received a text that I needed to report to the office immediately. I called to inquire what the emergency was, but the person downplayed it like it was just a regular expectation. I knew better because the source had proven that they were not truthful despite their position. Basically I said a prayer as I returned to the office and then I was advised that Human Resources (HR) wanted to meet with me. I met with the HR representatives and I was advised that my term would be ending on July 2, 2016 and it would not be renewed. They told me today would be my last day. Once I was given this information I literally shouted, "THANK YOU, JESUS!" and I cut a two-step praise dance. I sat down and advised the HR representatives to proceed. They actually were shocked and amazed because of my response was not downtrodden or of despair rather I had a peace and a praise on my lips and heart. They openly admitted that they never experienced that type of response. I assured them that God was my Source & Provider and he would take care of me.

As the HR representatives discussed what was occurring, I was pleasantly surprised to hear that although June 10, 2016 would be my last day, I would be on Administrative Leave with pay. My position was not any fault of my own. I was like God you are so awesome. I shared with my coworkers and I gave out my hugs then I was escorted out the building. My coworkers were tearful and some were angry. I told them that God had a bigger plan for my life and this company was only a chapter in my life not my final destination. I let them know that it was not over for me because God has Great things in store for me. I let the manager know when she escorted me out that she would be hearing about me for positive things in the community. I was not tearful at all and I had such a peace that it passed all understanding. I asked the Lord, 'Should I be crying?' I never did cry.

Well some of the things that took place while my job was paying me. I praise God for his favor: I was preparing for my Clinical Exam; I was able to attend my niece's and nephew's graduation closing exercise; I was able to attend my all doctor's appointments since my insurance was going to end; I was able to participate in dance rehearsals for a Kingdom Conference; I was able to travel to Memphis and attend the Unshakable Faith conference; I was able to join the gym; I was able to reconnect with my editor to let her know I was going to finish this book this summer; and more. It is too soon to reveal some of the other blessings that manifested during my time off. Definitely completing this book and starting my other books were a blessing in disguise. Truly God has been doing exceedingly and abundantly above all that I could ask or think.

Naturally, my situation looks bad but God confirmed that he was pleased with me and that I was right on track. As written in Isaiah 54:17, "No weapon formed against you shall be able to prosper." I am an Anointed Woman of God who is witnessing His daily provisions that it is not over until God says it is over. This project was an idea that came to pass. God had words flowing out of me like a river now here is a published book.

Fret not, the year is not over yet. There are still a few more days remaining in this year but you must move fast. Time out for procrastinating. Let's get the job done. I'm speaking to myself as well. IT'S NOT OVER SO: Reapply for that home loan, finish your book, complete that business plan, return to school, apply for that job, start your business, start that mentoring program, preach and teach the Word, write those songs, etc. Just do what He put in your spirit to do! Step out on faith and know according to Psalms 8:32 God will guide and teach you since He has plans to prosper you and give you hope and a future.

There are no limits through His grace and mercy. His favor is on your life. Walk it out. Step out and complete your dreams. I hope this book has encouraged you because it blessed and challenged me to Step Out and trust God.

Something to Think About: *What would you do if you knew there we NO Limits & All your resources & time needed were unlimited??? It's not over or too late!*

Journal Entry: His Stripes

"But it was our sins that did that to him, that ripped and tore and crushed him—our sins! He took the punishment, and that made us whole. Through his bruises we get healed." (Isaiah 53:5, MSG)

As I reflect back, I recall in the beginning of 2016 I noticed that I was feeling tired more often than usual. I figured that it was due to the cold winter months which normally slow most things down in the natural. My natural radar (gut) began to beep more frequently as the Spring arrived yet I was still feeling fatigued. Typically, I am an outgoing energizer most times, so to feel tired and weak was truly abnormal. As these symptoms continued, I finally decided to make a visit to my doctor. After visiting my doctor, I was reminded that I had an iron deficiency and a mild case of anemia. All of my close friends can attest that I crave ice constantly which is common for people with an iron deficiency. Honestly, I did not take this as a big deal. I was pretty much planning to add more vitamins into my diet and possibly take some Iron pill supplements.

On top of all of that, I was having challenges with my female organs to the point that my menstrual cycle was becoming irregular. My cycle was coming twice within one month among other weird things. I tried to start using birth control in hopes to regulate my menstrual cycle, however, I was not consistent with taking the pills. My problems continued and both my gynecologist and my primary care doctor were concerned. Thus, I made many visits to the doctors.

Overall I was fine but there were times during the day that my strength was completely zapped. I was feeling light headed and like I was about to pass out. I was having shortness of breath and wheezing and a consistent dry cough. This was happening so often that I started cancelling plans because I needed water and rest. Several times friends had to drive me home. During these moments, I would declare "By His Stripes I am Healed." After I would rest, I would feel better.

One day during a visit with my GYN, I shared with her that it was time for my annual mammogram. Amazingly, I was able to get an appointment the same day. I knew that it was God's favor to get an appointment that fast. After my results returned, I was advised to take a more thorough test because my breasts were dense. I declared and decreed, "I AM HEALED" despite this additional test. Then I had to get a biopsy and all of this occurred within a matters of weeks. I was told that the results of my biopsy would not take long. Again, I continued to confess that I am healed. Then I received messages from my doctor to call her because it was important. I attempted to call but I did not get through. I was scheduled for another appointment and I decided I talk. When I met with my doctor she told me that I had breast cancer in my right breast. I was not too shocked since I kept having follow up appointments. However, I was not accepting this report. I declared that I am Healed by the Blood of Jesus.

I was referred to an oncologist in Towson to discuss my situation. I must say that going to this doctor's office it was very warm and welcoming experience. There was a peaceful presence that I do not ever recall having in a typical doctor's office. The staff were very pleasant and attentive. After a number of different visits, the doctor reported that I have a noninvasive form of cancer. It was at Stage zero but it would require surgery to have it removed. He shared with me nobody wants any cancer but if one had to get it then this would be the ideal situation. I was listening to him, but in my mind, I was declaring that "By Your Stripes I am Healed" in Jesus name. I kept writing that scripture in my journal as well.

Initially, I did not plan to tell my close family and friends because I did not want them to worry about me. Eventually, I disclosed the news to two friends and asked them to pray and believe God for my healing as well. One of my spiritual advisors advised that I should not experience this alone but that I should share with those close to me who would stand in the gap, pray and support me. I opened up to my sister and she shared with her husband who had suspected that something was wrong with me since I had become fatigued more frequently and kept going to the doctors.

The day after I found out that I was diagnosed with breast cancer I was praying in the morning and listening on Youtube to be prepared for mime rehearsal. After the song was over, a different song by William Murphy's played and my spirit leaped and I started dancing to the song. As I worshipped God through dance, God spoke into my spirit and instructed me minister for a church within two days. About two weeks prior, I was asked to dance a church's 1st Anniversary Celebration, but initially I declined the request. I had planned to go out of town. However, my spirit leaped again and the Holy Ghost said that I needed to go to the church as part of my spiritual assignment. Thus, I changed my plans about going out of town. I told God

"Yes". My friend, was willing to do the dance with me but she had plans. I knew that God was telling me to go and so I had to be obedient. I did go and God did something miraculous.

For instance, I ministered with a member of the church who did mime while I danced. We met for the first time the day of the event. In preparation, we prayed, worshipped and humbled our spirits before God. Our worship connected us in the spirit realm and if you were to look at the video you would think that we rehearsed the dance. It was a fresh Holy Ghost download. After the guest preacher preached, the pastor of the church called for special prayer line to the altar, for healing from cancer. He stated that for the past three weeks God had spoken to him about healing. What is amazing and ironic is that during those past three weeks, I had several doctor's appointments regarding my breast. Needless to say, I was the first one in line. I had just written in my journal that I was healed prior to the altar call. I received it as confirmation for my healing. The Man of God spoke and declared that I was healed; I received it as well. I began to praise God in advance and worship Him. God spoke to my spirit that my obedience to minister in dance and willingness to change my personal plans, was bringing forth my healing and deliverance. I basked in God's presence and received the fullness of Joy. I still am taking one day at a time and thanking God for allowing me time to rest and travel with family and friends this summer.

I am still declaring my Healing by Faith despite any symptoms. I do not know when God is going to manifest my Healing but I will stand in Faith until He does. I continued to declare I am Healed. God is Jehovah Rapha my

Healer. DO YOU BELIEVE?

Update: I had to have another biopsy to examine if the doctor saw any additional cancer surrounding my breast. I was glad to report they did not.

The doctor recommended the surgery, I scheduled to have a lumpectomy on November 17, 2016 to remove the small cancer cells. What is amazing is that if my brother was alive, it would be his birthday. I shared earlier how his death brought forth my spiritual life. I still believe God that cancer will not take me out. I   still believe Him for healing.

Something to Think About: *The doctor may have given you a diagnosis and it may appear as if there is no hope. I want to encourage you to know that God is the Great Physician and He is a Healer. Let's believe the report of the Lord that you and n your family are Healed!*

{If you are a woman reading this, make sure you are receiving your routine check-ups with your doctors, including regular mammograms and self-breast examinations.}

Journal Entry: Write Those Books!

"Every Scripture is God-breathed...so that the man of God may be complete and proficient, well fitted and thoroughly equipped for every good work." (2 Timothy 3:16–17, AMP)

As I end this first book of faith, I urge you to do what God has instructed you to do. God spoke over my life years ago about to write but it was not until the last two years that He would not let me rest until I acted on it. And here it is alive and well. THANK YOU JESUS! I do not want you to wait 17 years to push out your dreams. With God, you really can do it. If you are an author in the making, let your story be revealed. Let it unfold and allow the world to be amazed by your resilience and strength. You have made it through storms, trials, and rain. The devil thought your life was over and you were going to give up. It was tough but you held on.

Therefore, PUSH out those babies! Do not allow them to be stillborn. God has already equipped you for the task at hand. Use the resources you have and let God make up the difference.

Step out on Faith! Dare to Dream! If you can dream it, then it is possible.

I look forward to hearing your story and how this book compelled you to go forth.

Something to Think About: *What is your DREAM?*

Closing Inspiration

Applied Scripture

"Every scripture is God-breathed...so that the
man of God may be complete and proficient, well
fitted and thoroughly equipped for every good
work."
(2 Timothy 3:16–17, AMP)

You are equipped to do what God is directing you to
do! Listen and obey His voice. You can do ALL through
Christ Jesus who strengthens you. He will align you with
the right people to assist and encourage you once you
step out on faith. There will be days of uncertainty, but
still trust God to make every provision you need. Do not
give up- even when the odds to be appear against you.
"Attitude determines your altitude." Some problems and
challenges are hidden miracles for God to work out on
your behalf. If I can do it in spite of my mistakes and fail-
ures, then you can as well. God is no respecter of persons
(Acts 10:34). This book took 4 years to write, but I do not
want you to take that long to fulfill your DREAM. The Time
is NOW!

A PRAYER FOR TODAY

"FATHER, THANK YOU FOR EQUIPPING ME. THANK YOU FOR EMPOWERING ME. HELP
ME TO STAY FOCUSED ON YOUR WORD AND YOUR PLAN FOR ME TODAY. I BLESS YOU AND
HONOR YOU ALONE IN JESUS' NAME. AMEN."

Appendices

Scripture References

"Every scripture is God-breathed...so that the man of God may be complete and proficient, well fitted and thoroughly equipped for every good work." (2 Timothy 3:16–17, AMP) .....

47626156R00060

Made in the USA
Middletown, DE
09 June 2019